THE
INFOGRAPHIC
GUIDE TO
GRAMMAR

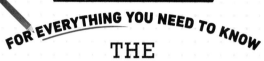

A VISUAL REFERENCE

FOR EVERYTHING YOU NEED TO KNOW

THE

INFOGRAPHIC

GUIDE TO

GRAMMAR

JARA KERN

Adams Media

New York   London   Toronto   Sydney   New Delhi

Adams Media
An Imprint of Simon & Schuster, Inc.
100 Technology Center Drive
Stoughton, MA 02072

First Adams Media trade paperback edition April 2020

ADAMS MEDIA and colophon are trademarks of Simon & Schuster.

For information about special discounts for bulk purchases, please contact Simon & Schuster Special Sales at 1-866-506-1949 or business@simonandschuster.com.

The Simon & Schuster Speakers Bureau can bring authors to your live event. For more information or to book an event contact the Simon & Schuster Speakers Bureau at 1-866-248-3049 or visit our website at www.simonspeakers.com.

Interior design by Sylvia McArdle, Julia Jacintho, Harini Rajagopalan, and Priscilla Yuen
Interior images © 123RF; Getty Images

Manufactured in the United States of America

5 2021

ISBN 978-1-5072-1238-7
ISBN 978-1-5072-1239-4 (ebook)

CONTENTS

CHAPTER 1

PARTS OF SPEECH

→ **Nouns** 14

→ **Adjectives** 16

→ **Verbs** 18

→ **Adverbs** 20

→ **Verb Tenses** 22

→ **Regular vs. Irregular Verbs** 24

→ **Pronouns** 26

→ **Prepositions & Prepositional Phrases** 28

→ **Conjunctions** 30

→ **Interjections!** 32

CHAPTER 2

SENTENCE STRUCTURE

Sentence Functions   36

Subjects and Predicates   38

Subject-Verb Agreement   40

Compound Subjects   42

Complements   44

Phrases   46

Clauses   48

Restrictive Clauses & Non-Restrictive Clauses   50

Parallelism and Logical Sentences   52

CHAPTER 3

PUNCTUATION

→ **Capitalization** 56

→ **Ending a Sentence** 58

→ **Apostrophes & Contractions** 60

→ **Commas** 62

→ **Quotation Marks** 64

→ **Colons & Semicolons** 66

→ **Hyphens, Em Dashes, & En Dashes** 68

→ **Parentheses** 70

→ **Brackets** 72

→ **Bold, Italics, and Underlining** 74

→ **Ellipses** 76

→ **The Slash** 78

→ **Abbreviations & Acronyms** 80

CHAPTER 4

WRITING STYLE

Identifying Your Purpose and Audience   84

Active & Passive Voice   86

Using Transitional Words and Phrases   88

Paragraph Structure   90

Fixing Repetition and Introducing Variety   92

Foreign Words & Phrases   94

Slang & Dialect   96

Improving Writing   98

Style Guides: A Brief Overview   100

CHAPTER 5

COMMON MISTAKES

Clichés, Generalizations, Platitudes, and Jargon   104

Commonly Confused Words   106

Who & Whom   108

More Common Mistakes   110

Commonly Misused Phrases   112

Modifier Problems   114

Run-On Sentences and Wordiness   116

Double Negatives   118

Fussy Grammar   120

INTRODUCTION

English is a challenging language to master, even for native speakers. Why? Well, for starters, it's been spiced by many dialects and regional variations. It has also borrowed freely from many other languages. Even today, new words and expressions frequently enter the language. One of the most challenging parts of the English language is the grammar: the standard set of rules for spelling, punctuation, sentence structure, and word use.

English grammar is difficult to grasp thanks to its many layers of rules. That's where this book can help—it will lay out the basic rules of grammar (along with tricks to help you avoid common mistakes) in fifty easy-to-understand infographic spreads. With *The Infographic Guide to Grammar*, you will learn all about subject-verb agreement, sentence structure, interjections, complements, punctuation, and more. You'll also discover the right way to use commonly confused words, like *there/ their/ they're*, and find out what clauses are and how to use them. This book will help you understand the how and why behind English grammar, giving you more confidence in your writing and speaking.

Whether you're a new English learner, a student brushing up on your grammar lessons, an aspiring writer, or a grammar nerd, *The Infographic Guide to Grammar* teaches you everything you need and want to know about grammar in a fun, illustrated format.

CHAPTER 1

PARTS OF SPEECH

→ Nouns 14

→ Adjectives 16

→ Verbs 18

→ Adverbs 20

→ Verb Tenses 22

→ Regular vs. Irregular Verbs 24

→ Pronouns 26

→ Prepositions & Prepositional Phrases 28

→ Conjunctions 30

→ Interjections! 32

NOUNS

PEOPLE

PLACES

THINGS

Think of nouns as the CELEBRITIES of the grammar world: Sentences are really all about them. Nouns can be subjects or objects—or even both.

DID YOU KNOW?

Noun comes from the word *nōmen*, Latin for "name."

While all nouns serve as labels for **people, places, things,** or ideas, there are some specific terms for different types.

COMMON NOUN

Non-specific person, place, or thing
Examples:
grandmother, city

PROPER NOUN

Specific person, place, or thing
Examples: Grandma Jane, New York City

CONCRETE NOUN

Noun you experience with your senses
Examples: sunshine, song

ABSTRACT NOUN

Noun that is an idea, feeling, or state of being
Examples: pride, exhaustion

COUNT NOUN

Individual noun you can count
Examples: horse, dollar

NON-COUNT NOUN

Noun used when you can't count
Examples: food, rain

COLLECTIVE NOUN

Noun that represents a collection or group
Examples: family, hive

POSSESSIVE NOUN

Noun used to show ownership
Examples: father's key, people's ideas

 GOOD TO KNOW:

Attributive Nouns: Nouns can act as adjectives to describe other nouns. Think of *chicken soup*, for example. Both words are nouns, but here *chicken* is being used to modify *soup*. In this case, *chicken* is an attributive noun.

ADJECTIVES

An **adjective** modifies a noun or pronoun to give more information about a person, place, or thing.

— IDENTIFYING ADJECTIVES —

ADJECTIVES ANSWER:

1. WHICH ONE?

2. WHAT KIND?

3. HOW MANY?

DID YOU KNOW?

Adjective comes from the Middle English *adjectif*, borrowed from Anglo-French and Late Latin.

– TYPES OF ADJECTIVES –

ARTICLES

- Point out or refer to a person, place, or thing as specific or unspecific; can be definite or indefinite
- **Definite Example:** *the*
- **Indefinite Examples:** *a, an*

DEMONSTRATIVE

- Distinguishes the person, place, or thing being described
- **Examples:** *this, that, these, those*

INDEFINITE

- Used to describe an entire group or indicate lack of familiarity or specificity
- **Examples:** *all, another, any, both, each, less, neither, some,* etc.

POSSESSIVE

- Describes who has or owns something
- **Examples:** *my, your, his, her, its, our, their*

INTERROGATIVE

- Begins a question
- **Examples:** *what, which, whose*

PROPER

- Formed from a proper noun, and therefore always begins with a capital letter
- **Examples:** *Thai food, French terry*

VERBS

Describing an Action or State

A **verb** is a word that indicates an action or a state of being. It tells the story of the sentence.

WHAT KIND OF VERB?

ACTION VERBS

Verbs that show movement or change.
The turtle dived into the water.

VERBS OF BEING

Verbs that express a state, usually a variation of "to be."
The boy was tired.

LINKING VERBS

These connect a sentence's parts—and are usually forms of "be" in disguise. If you can swap the verb without changing the sentence's meaning, it's a linking verb.
The coffee tasted sweet. = The coffee was sweet.

AUXILIARY VERBS

These helpers express more about the main verb.
You can join the club.

TRANSITIVE VS. INTRANSITIVE VERBS

Action verbs can be either transitive or intransitive depending on whether or not there is a noun receiving the action (also known as a **direct object**).

TRANSITIVE

Eat, paint, kick

Example:
He _kicked_ (verb) the ball (direct object).

INTRANSITIVE

Sit, sneeze, arrive

Example: They _arrived_ (verb) at the party (no direct object).

Some verbs can be both **transitive** and **intransitive**:

Transitive:
He _closed_ the door.

Intransitive:
The door _closed_.

 GOOD TO KNOW:

Forms of "Be"

IS   WAS   BEING

AM   ARE   WERE   BEEN

ADVERBS

Mighty Modifiers

An **adverb** tells us more about a verb, adjective, or even another adverb (yes, English is complicated). The fastest way to spot an adverb is to look for a word ending in *-ly*, though there are exceptions—like *fast, never, well, very, now,* and *quite*.

 GOOD TO KNOW:

DOUBLE DUTY

Some words are used as both adjectives and adverbs—without modification. These include *early, daily, weekly, hourly, fast, half, straight, just, late, low, most, clear,* and *clean*.

ADVERBS ANSWER:

7 TO WHAT EXTENT?

1 HOW?

6 HOW OFTEN?

2 WHEN?

5 HOW MUCH?

3 WHERE?

4 UNDER WHAT CIRCUMSTANCES?

ADVERBS IN ACTION

Modifying a verb: *My dad drove __slowly__ through traffic.*

Modifying an adjective: *The sun was __extremely__ bright.*

Modifying another adverb: *Cheetahs can run __remarkably__ fast.*

VERB TENSES

Verb tenses relate action to time, telling us whether something has occurred in the past, is happening right now, or will take place in the future. These three main tenses are then subcategorized further, for a total of twelve possible tenses.

 GOOD TO KNOW:

QUICK SELF-CHECK TIPS

Not sure you're using the correct verb form for the tense? Try these tips:

Use **"Yesterday"** to start your **past** tense sentence.	Use **"Today"** to start your **present** tense sentence.	Use **"Tomorrow"** to start your **future** tense sentence.

Why 12 Tenses?

In English, there are only two ways to form a tense from the verb alone: the past and the present. For more detail, you must add a form of *have*, *be*, or *will*—called a **helping** or an **auxiliary verb**. Let's take a look.

THE 12 ENGLISH VERB TENSES

PARTICULAR USE				
	Simple	Progressive	Perfect	Perfect Progressive
	For an action that is **usual** or **repeated**	For an action that is **ongoing**	For an action that is **completed**	For an ongoing action that will be **completed at a definite time**
PAST	ate	was/were eating	had eaten	had been eating
PRESENT	eat	am/is/are eating	has/have eaten	has/have been eating
FUTURE	will/shall eat	will be eating	will have eaten	will have been eating

IN ACTION

REGULAR VS.

EXCEPTIONS TO THE RULE

As if learning about tenses wasn't complicated enough, the English language stumps learners with **irregular verbs**. In fact, some of our most common verbs are irregular!

All verbs, both regular and irregular, have

5 FORMS:

INFINITIVE
SIMPLE PRESENT
SIMPLE PAST
PRESENT PARTICIPLE
PAST PARTICIPLE

REGULAR VERBS

To form the simple past or past participle forms, add -*d* or -*ed* to the infinitive (base form) of the verb.

Example:
work—worked

IRREGULAR VERBS

These verbs undergo significant changes between the infinitive, simple past, and past participle forms.

Example:
go—went, gone

IRREGULAR VERBS

MOST COMMON IRREGULAR VERBS

When learning English, speakers memorize most of the 200+ irregular verbs and their simple past and past participle forms. Some of the most common include:

INFINITIVE	SIMPLE PAST	PAST PARTICIPLE
be	was, were	been
bring	brought	brought
do	did	done
feel	felt	felt
get	got	gotten, got
go	went	gone
lead	led	led
run	ran	run
say	said	said
see	saw	seen

 GOOD TO KNOW:

Why Do We Have Irregular Verbs?

Most irregular verbs come from Old English, the earliest spoken version of the English language, used in Great Britain before 1100. Newer verbs are borrowed from other languages or are converted from nouns—and tend to be regular.

PRONOUNS

NOUN SUBSTITUTES

A **pronoun** is a word that takes the place of a noun to add variety and avoid repetition.

PRONOUN POWER

Which sentence sounds more natural?

Jack came into the room, picked up Jack's pencil, sat down at Jack's desk, and began to work on Jack's final exam.

Jack came into the room, picked up his pencil, sat down at his desk, and began to work on his final exam.

 **GOOD TO KNOW:**

Singular *They/Their*

The words *they*, *their*, *them*, and *themselves* are sometimes used as singular pronouns when talking about someone whose gender isn't specified, or someone who chooses not to use *he* or *she*. While the gender-neutral purpose is new, the use of the singular *they* is not: The *Oxford English Dictionary* traces the use as far back as 1375!

PRONOUN CLASSIFICATIONS

 PERSONAL

Represent people, places, or things
- I, me, you, he, him, she, her, it, we, us, they, them
- *I came to see you today.*

 POSSESSIVE

Show ownership
- Mine, yours, his, hers, ours, theirs
- *That car is ours.*

 DEMONSTRATIVE

Point to something
- This, that, these, those
- *This is her lunchbox.*

 RELATIVE

Relate one part of the sentence to another
- Who, whom, which, that, whose
- *The girl who was sick went home.*

 REFLEXIVE

Emphasize or reflect back to someone or something else
- Myself, yourself, yourselves, himself, herself, itself, ourselves, themselves
- *You must ask yourself what you want.*

 INDEFINITE

Make non-specific references
- All, another, any, anybody/anyone, anything, each, everybody/everyone, everything, few, many, nobody, none, one, several, some, somebody/someone
- *Nobody was home.*

 RECIPROCAL

Express mutual action
- Each other, one another
- *They talked to each other on the way.*

 INTERROGATIVE

Ask a question
- Who, whom, what
- *What can I do if that happens?*

PREPOSITIONS & PREPOSITIONAL PHRASES

Linking Words

A **preposition** connects a noun or a pronoun to another word in the sentence to show the relationship between the two. It often indicates the position of something in the sentence—*under*, *over*, *above*, *below*, or *beneath*.

SPOTTING PREPOSITIONS

They sat <u>in</u> the corner.
In is a preposition connecting ***they*** and ***corner***.

Jack and Jill went <u>up</u> the hill.
Up is a preposition joining ***went*** and ***hill***.

GOOD TO KNOW:

ENDING SENTENCES?

Should you end a sentence with a preposition? You can. While some grammar sticklers may frown upon ending a sentence this way in formal written English—such as a book or an article—the practice is perfectly acceptable. In fact, when speaking, people often do:

Whom are you talking with?/What was that about?

COMMON PREPOSITIONS

Look for words like:

about	before	during	over	up
above	behind	for	since	upon
across	between	from	through	with
after	but	into	toward	within
against	by	like	under	without
among	despite	of	until	
around	down	onto		
at				

WHEN IS A PREPOSITION *NOT* A PREPOSITION?

All prepositions must be used in prepositional phrases, which consist of the preposition and a noun or pronoun (and sometimes adjectives and adverbs). If the word is used alone, it's an adjective or adverb. See the difference?

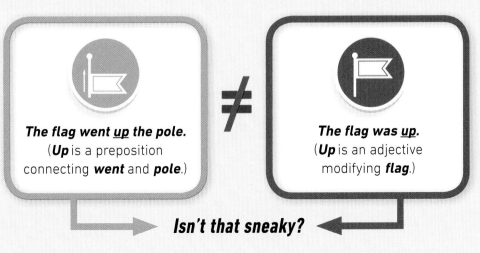

The flag went <u>up the pole</u>.
(***Up*** is a preposition connecting ***went*** and ***pole***.)

≠

The flag was <u>up</u>.
(***Up*** is an adjective modifying ***flag***.)

Isn't that sneaky?

CONJUNCTIONS
Connectors

Think of **conjunctions** as words that join two parts of a sentence together. There are three types: *coordinating*, *correlative*, and *subordinating*. Let's get to know them.

Coordinating Conjunctions

Remember the seven coordinating conjunctions easily using the mnemonic **FANBOYS**, an acronym of *for*, *and*, *nor*, *but*, *or*, *yet*, and *so*.

Examples:

I bought apples (and) bananas.

I waited (for) the green arrow (and) turned left.

Correlative Conjunctions

These conjunctions come in pairs—both must appear in the sentence for it to work. They include:

Examples:

I would rather *bike* than *walk.*
Neither *the boy* nor *the girl knew the answer.*

Subordinating Conjunctions

These sneaky conjunctions are used at the beginning of **dependent clauses**, sections of a sentence that add detail or indicate cause but that cannot stand alone. Look for (among others):

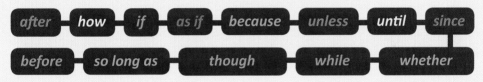

Examples:

Because *she was late, she missed the train.*
After *I ate, I felt better.*

STARTING A SENTENCE?

While it was once considered incorrect to start a sentence with a sub-ordinating conjunction, it is now considered OK. And that's a good thing, as doing so can enhance flow between sentences and add variety.

INTERJECTIONS!

Expressing Emotion

WHAT?
REALLY?
You need help on
interjections?
NO WAY!

Interjections
are words or phrases that
express surprise, displeasure,
and other strong emotions.
They often stand alone, and
you'll use them in spoken
dialogue much more than in
written communication.

Hooray!

Congratulations!

Yuck!

Oops!

Ouch!

Nice!

Oh no!

PUNCTUATE!

Hey! Looking for oomph? Use an exclamation point!

Whoa. Feeling something milder? Opt for a period.

USE SPARINGLY

Interjections are meant to surprise and interrupt; exercise moderation when using them.

SALTY INTERJECTIONS

Many off-color interjections—OK, curse words—not suitable for print use non-letter symbols to stand in for the words.

That $@# car wouldn't start again!*

 GOOD TO KNOW:

FOR INTERJECTIONS ONLY

Any part of speech can be used as an interjection, such as *Good!* (adjective), *Idiot!* (noun), and *Go!* (verb). Some words, however, are exclusively interjections, such as *Ouch!* and *Oops!*

CHAPTER 2

SENTENCE STRUCTURE

→ **Sentence Functions** 36

→ **Subjects and Predicates** 38

→ **Subject-Verb Agreement** 40

→ **Compound Subjects** 42

→ **Complements** 44

→ **Phrases** 46

→ **Clauses** 48

→ **Restrictive Clauses & Non-Restrictive Clauses** 50

→ **Parallelism and Logical Sentences** 52

SENTENCE FUNCTIONS

A **sentence** is made up of one or more words and expresses a complete thought in a statement, question, request, command, or exclamation.

 GOOD TO KNOW:

FRAGMENTS

A sentence fragment looks like a complete sentence but isn't, often because it is a subordinate clause. Let's take this example:

▶ *Because he was hungry.*

Here, the first word is capitalized and the clause ends with a period, but it cannot stand alone. A correct, complete sentence needs an independent clause:

▶ *Because he was hungry, the small boy ordered a large hamburger.*

Sentence Types

There are **4** categories of sentences: simple, compound, **complex**, and compound-complex. Using all four types and mixing them up gives your writing variety.

1

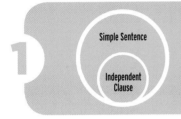

SIMPLE

Expresses one complete thought with one independent clause and no dependent clause.

The small boy ordered a large hamburger.

2

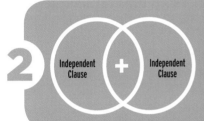

COMPOUND

Has two independent clauses—joined by **and** (or another conjunction or a semicolon)—and no dependent clause.

The small boy ordered a large hamburger, and the server brought him ketchup.

3

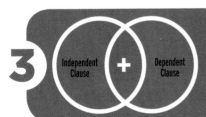

COMPLEX

Has one independent clause and one or more dependent clauses.

Because he was hungry, the small boy ordered a large hamburger.

4

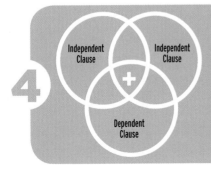

COMPOUND-COMPLEX

Has at least two independent clauses and one or more dependent clauses.

Because he was hungry, the small boy ordered a large hamburger, and the server brought him ketchup.

SUBJECTS AND PREDICATES

Sentences can be very short or very long. At a minimum, though, they must contain a **SUBJECT** and a **PREDICATE** and be able to stand on their own.

SUBJECT: What the Sentence Is About

The complete **subject** is the person, place, or thing that serves as the topic of the sentence—along with all the words that describe it.

To locate the subject, ask yourself: "Who or what is the sentence about?"

FINDING THE SUBJECT

PREDICATE:
Action, State of Being, or Condition

The complete **predicate** is what the person, place, or thing is do-ing or what condition it is in—along with all the words that modify it.

Imperative Sentences

Go find my shoes.

Where's the subject in this sentence? Some imperative sentences—those that express commands or requests—drop the "you" in the subject. The meaning is really:

<u>You</u> go find my shoes.

The young woman **sprinted.**

Here, "the young woman" is the subject; "sprinted" is the predicate.

SUBJECT-VERB AGREEMENT

There is only one rule about subject-verb agreement:

You must make verbs agree with their subjects in number and in person. Of course, this is English, so this rule can be tricky to follow.

 GOOD TO KNOW:

TRICKY INDEFINITE PRONOUNS

Here are two key rules about indefinite pronouns:

1 *Each*, *everybody*, *everyone*, *everything*, and *no one* are **singular** and take a singular verb.

2 *All*, *any*, *most*, and *some* can be **singular** or **plural** depending on what they are referring to: the verb form should match the subject in number.

SUBJECT-VERB AGREEMENT CHEAT SHEET

Subject Complication	Singular or Plural Verb?	Example
Titles of books, movies, and songs	Always singular	• The *Fellowship of the Ring* is a long movie.
Prepositions and prepositional phrases	Depends—ignore the preposition or prepositional phrase to make agreement easier	• The box of Popsicles was in the freezer. (Box = singular— ignore "of Popsicles")
Indefinite pronouns	Singular pronoun, singular verb; plural pronoun, plural verb	• Somebody owns that cabin. • A few of us own that cabin.
Amount—as a single unit, such as time, money, food, fractions, or volume	Always singular	• Ten dollars is the price. • Half of the pie is uneaten.
Collective nouns	Singular for collective noun conveying unity; plural for collective noun conveying plurality	• The United States is a big country. • The faculty were in agreement.

WHAT ABOUT *SCISSORS* AND *PANTS*?

Using *pants, trousers, shears, spectacles, glasses, tongs,* or *scissors* alone? Choose a plural verb: *The pants are on sale.* Add the word "pair" and you need to use a singular verb: *The pair of pants is on sale.*

COMPOUND SUBJECTS

TWO OR MORE SUBJECTS? SIMPLE RULES OF THUMB

Compound subjects consist of two or more individual nouns or noun phrases connected by **"and"** or **"or"** to form a single, longer noun phrase. They're tricky because they can confuse subject-verb agreement.

 **GOOD TO KNOW:**

EXCEPTION: If the subjects are joined by "and" and they can be thought of as a unit, use a singular verb.
Example: *Is spaghetti and meatballs on the menu?*

MAKE IT EASIER BY FOLLOWING
4 SIMPLE RULES:

1

SUBJECTS JOINED BY "AND" TAKE A PLURAL VERB.

Why?: Using "and" makes them plural.
Example: *The student and the teacher play the game.*

2

SINGULAR SUBJECTS JOINED BY "OR" OR "NOR" TAKE A SINGULAR VERB.

Why?: You're referring to one or the other, not both.
Example: *Neither the teacher nor his student plays the game.*

3

PLURAL SUBJECTS JOINED BY "OR" OR "NOR" TAKE A PLURAL VERB.

Why?: Both subjects are plural.
Example: *Either the students or the teacher plays the game.*

4

VERBS AGREE WITH THE SUBJECT CLOSEST TO THEM.

But: Only if you have one singular and one plural subject.
Examples: *The students or the teacher plays the game.*
The teacher or the students play the game.

COMPLEMENTS

While some sentences contain only a subject and a verb, others use more words to make things clearer, tell a story, or ask a question. These additional sentence components are called **complements**, and they fall into five categories.

DIRECT OBJECT

A direct object receives the action of the verb and is usually a noun or pronoun. Ask yourself "Who or what?" to find it.

EXAMPLE:
Mom drank coffee.

> *Coffee* is the **direct object**.

OBJECT COMPLEMENT

An object complement follows and modifies or refers to a direct object. It can be a noun, pronoun, adjective, or phrase.

EXAMPLE:
I painted my bedroom yellow.

> *Bedroom* is the **direct object**, and *yellow* is the **object complement**.

44

3

INDIRECT OBJECT

An indirect object comes between the verb and the direct object and answers the question "To whom?" or "For whom?"

EXAMPLE:

Melissa tossed Anthony the ball.

Anthony is the **indirect object**, and *ball* is the **direct object**.

4

PREDICATE ADJECTIVE

A predicate adjective is an adjective that comes after a linking verb (e.g., *to be, appear, feel, remain, taste, stay*) to describe the subject, answering the question "What?"

EXAMPLE:

The peach tasted sour.

Sour is the **predicate adjective**, and *tasted* is the **linking verb**.

5

PREDICATE NOMINATIVE

A predicate nominative is a noun or pronoun that also comes after a linking verb, but it renames the subject and answers the question "Who?" or "What?"

EXAMPLE:

That tall man is my uncle.

Uncle is the **predicate nominative**.

PHRASES

A **phrase** is a group of words that adds detail to a sentence but doesn't have a subject and a verb. Phrases can be part of sentences but cannot stand alone.

ADDING DETAIL: 5 TYPES OF PHRASES

1

Adjective Phrases

These phrases give more detail about a noun, and they are usually found right after the word or words they modify.

Example:
A few kids from my school will be coming over Saturday.

From my school is an **adjective phrase** modifying kids.

2

Adverb Phrases

These words modify a verb and appear right after it.

Example: We will play on the field.

On the field is an **adverb phrase** telling us where we will play.

GERUNDS: A **gerund** is a present participle that acts as a noun (subject). Try this example: *Dancing made us happy.* Here, *dancing* is the subject, and *made* is the verb.

3 ✦

Participial Phrases

Participial phrases using a present participle are formed by adding *-ing* to a verb, and act as adjectives.

Example: (Reaching high,) Janie caught the fly ball.

> Reaching high is the **participial phrase**.

4 ✦

Infinitive Phrases

An infinitive is "to + verb," and this construction can act as a subject.

Example: (To make partner) is his big goal.

> To make partner is the **infinitive phrase**.

5 ✦

Appositive Phrases

An appositive is a noun (or, rarely, a pronoun) that gives more information about another noun or pronoun.

Example: My older sister, (the really tall girl,) was late to class.

> The really tall girl is the **appositive phrase** further describing *my older sister*.

CLAUSES

Complex Phrases

A **clause** is a phrase with a subject and a verb and any complements the verb requires. Depending on the type, it may or may not be able to stand alone as a sentence.

Independent Clauses

Because they express a complete thought, these clauses can stand alone. Two or more together can be joined by a conjunction in a sentence.

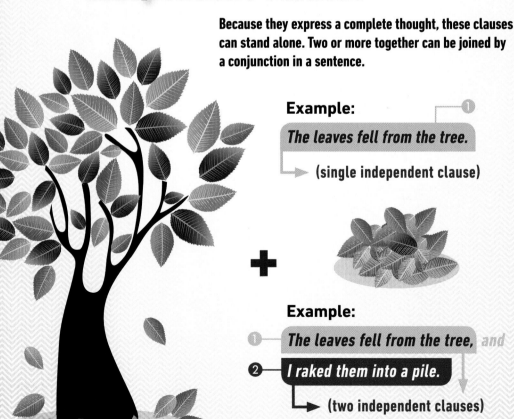

Example:

The leaves fell from the tree.

(single independent clause)

+

Example:

① *The leaves fell from the tree, and*

② *I raked them into a pile.*

(two independent clauses)

PUNCTUATION

Independent clauses connected by *and, but, for, or, nor, so,* or *yet* should be separated by a comma. Independent clauses without a conjunction take a semicolon.

▶ **Examples:**

It was windy, so the leaves fell from the trees.

It was windy; the leaves fell from the trees.

Subordinate Clauses

Also known as dependent clauses, these clauses do not make sense by themselves. Look for *because, when, who, whom,* and other conjunctions or relative pronouns.

Example:

Because it was windy,

the leaves fell from the tree.

Because it was windy
DOESN'T MAKE SENSE ALONE;
it needs to connect with
the rest of the sentence.

RESTRICTIVE & CLAUSES

Categorizing Clauses: Necessary or Not?

Clauses can also be categorized by whether or not they are necessary to the meaning of a sentence. After all, sometimes we need more detail, and sometimes we don't.

Also known as an essential clause or defining clause, a **restrictive clause** is essential to the sentence's meaning.

▶ EXAMPLE

*The sandwich **that I just purchased** is on the counter in the kitchen.*

The restrictive clause, ***that I just purchased***, distinguishes the sandwich from any and all others.

NON–RESTRICTIVE CLAUSES

Non-restrictive clauses could be omitted from a sentence without changing its meaning.

▶ EXAMPLE

*The car, **which has only 50,000 miles on it**, needs a new timing belt.*

Omitting **which has only 50,000 miles on it** does not fundamentally change the sentence's meaning; the clause is non-restrictive.

 GOOD TO KNOW:

THAT vs. WHICH: In general, the word **that** introduces restrictive clauses, and the word **which** begins non-restrictive clauses. Non-restrictive clauses are typically set off by commas, while restrictive clauses are not.

51

PARALLELISM AND LOGICAL SENTENCES

Conveying Thoughts Clearly

Sometimes you must organize related thoughts, show that actions are sequential, or build to a climax to make a point. These cases call for **parallelism**, which means using the same grammatical structure for all the similar parts of a sentence. Here's how.

USE A CONSISTENT VOICE

Ensure that you're using a consistent voice (active or passive) and an introduction to each clause in a series.

I was worried that the test would be too hard, I would not be prepared, and my pencil would be forgotten at home.

I was worried that I would forget my pencil, I would not be prepared, and the test would be too hard.

WATCH YOUR VERB TENSE AGREEMENT

Don't mix verb tenses.

 I washed, dried, and was curling my hair.

 I washed, dried, and curled my hair.

SIMPLIFY ITEMS IN PAIRS OR IN A SERIES

Present actions, attributes, or items in a series in a simple and coherent way.

 Jennifer is very kind and is very organized.

 Jennifer is very kind and organized.

INCLUDE THE RIGHT WORDS

Be sure to include all the words you need in the sentence.

 To learn more, I talked to the girl and neighbor.

 To learn more, I talked to the girl and her neighbor.

KEEP THINGS IN ORDER OF EMPHASIS OR TIMING

Place actions in chronological order or items with differing degrees of importance in increasing order.

 Use equipment properly or risk death or injury.

 Use equipment properly or risk injury or death.

CHAPTER 3

PUNCTUATION

→ **Capitalization**   56

→ **Ending a Sentence**   58

→ **Apostrophes & Contractions**   60

→ **Commas**   62

→ **Quotation Marks**   64

→ **Colons & Semicolons**   66

→ **Hyphens, Em Dashes, & En Dashes**   68

→ **Parentheses**   70

→ **Brackets**   72

→ **Bold, Italics, and Underlining**   74

→ **Ellipses**   76

→ **The Slash**   78

→ **Abbreviations & Acronyms**   80

CAPITALIZATION
Using Uppercase

When you **capitalize**, you write a word with the first letter in uppercase and the remaining letters in lowercase.

General Capitalization Guidelines:

CAPITALIZE...

...the first word of a sentence and every first word after a period, question mark, or exclamation point.

Example: *Hello! My name is Joe.*

...proper nouns; don't capitalize the "the" preceding proper nouns.

Example: *I went to the Grand Canyon.*

...days of the week, months of the year, and names of holidays.

Example: *I am visiting on Friday, November 29, the day after Thanksgiving.*

DON'T CAPITALIZE...

...the names of seasons.

Example: *I'm planning to go camping this summer.*

...people's first and last names and their nicknames.

Example: *This is my friend James; we call him Jim.*

...family names when used immediately before, or instead of, a personal name.

Example: *Did Mom already arrive? Aunt Ann loves the pie my mom planned on bringing. Yes, your mom is by the dessert table.*

...the names of brands, companies, and institutions, such as schools and associations.

Example: *I think that Nike sneakers are the most popular shoes at Memorial Middle School.*

...the names of streets and roads; cities; states and provinces; countries; and natural and human-made landmarks.

Example: *I live in New Hampshire, not far from Mount Washington.*

DON'T CAPITALIZE...

...words like "country" if they're used before the proper noun.

Example: *The country of Wales is my favorite place to visit in the United Kingdom.*

...titles when they are used before names or as a form of direct address.

Example: *The players learned how to fish from Captain Mike.*

Example: *Put me in, Coach!*

DON'T CAPITALIZE...

...a title if it follows a name or is used instead of a name.

Example: *Mike, the captain, spotted the whale first.*

...titles when they are used as descriptive terms rather than as part of the name.

Example: *The captain, Mike Torrez, brought us in early to avoid the storm.*

...the first word in a quote if it forms a complete sentence.

Example: *The scientist said, "The planet Earth is about 25,000 miles in circumference."*

DON'T CAPITALIZE...

...the first letter of a quote that is an incomplete sentence.

Example: *In the full report, she explains that the Earth rotates "about one thousand miles per hour."*

ENDING A SENTENCE

Punctuation Choices

When ending a sentence, you have three choices: a period, a question mark, or an exclamation point.

THE PERIOD

Use a period when your sentence states a fact or makes a command.

Examples:

- *My best friend works as an elementary school teacher.*
- *Be ready when I arrive at your house.*

THE QUESTION MARK

A question mark shows doubt in a sentence or conveys that a question is being asked.

Examples:

- *What did you say?*
- *Can you be ready when I arrive?*

THE EXCLAMATION POINT

An exclamation point expresses strong feelings or tells you something extraordinary happened.

Examples:

- *You don't say!*
- *She actually called him!*

APOSTROPHES &

The **apostrophe** can cause confusion, but it doesn't have to. Three basic situations require an apostrophe:

1 MAKING A CONTRACTION

The use of an apostrophe tells you at least one letter was omitted as two words were joined, creating a contraction.

▸ *Do not* becomes *don't*.

▸ *He would* becomes *he'd*.

2 INDICATING POSSESSION

Use an apostrophe to indicate ownership.

▸ *Diana's car is parked on the street.*

▸ *The teacher's desk is up front.*

3 FORMING A PLURAL (rare)

Use an apostrophe to make a word plural when readers would be confused by an "s" alone.

▸ *Count by 2's.*

▸ *Dot your i's and cross your t's.*

CONTRACTIONS

Apostrophes can be confusing when it comes to family names.

Are you talking about something that several people collectively own? Use an apostrophe after (not before) the "s" that makes the word plural.

▶ *The Smiths' car is there.*

Are you sending holiday greetings? Do not use an apostrophe; use the plural form of your name.

▶ *With love, from the Smiths.*

GOOD TO KNOW:

ITS VS. IT'S

When do you use the possessive pronoun *its* or the contraction *it's*? Try out the sentence with "it is" to choose correctly. **Which one?:** *Its raining tonight* or *It's raining tonight*. *It's* is correct because the sentence is: *It is raining tonight.*

COMMAS

CREATING A PAUSE

The **comma** creates a slight pause in a sentence and helps readers understand how items relate to one another.

 GOOD TO KNOW:

SERIAL COMMA: Known as the *serial*, *Oxford*, or *Harvard comma*, this use separates the last two items in a series. Depending on your instructor, audience, or company, its use may be optional.

Serial comma: *I bought apples, bananas, and oranges.*

No serial comma: *I bought apples, bananas and oranges.*

COMMAS WITH A SERIES

Use a comma to separate items in a series and to eliminate confusion about how many or which one.

Which sentence is easier to understand and does more to describe the subject?

▶ *Her favorite flavors of ice cream were mint chocolate and strawberry.*

▶ *Her favorite flavors of ice cream were mint chocolate, and strawberry.*

In the first sentence, it seems like there are only two flavors, while in the second it becomes clear that we're talking about three flavors.

COMMAS WITH CLAUSES

Use a comma to separate the two clauses of a compound sentence when they are connected by *for*, *and*, *nor*, *but*, *or*, *yet*, and *so* (our mnemonic FANBOYS).

▶ *The light turned green, and he hit the gas.*

Use commas to enclose clauses that aren't essential to the sentence's meaning.

▶ *The tires, which I've had for three years, need to be replaced.*

COMMAS IN DATES

Use a comma after the month and date, and after the year if the sentence continues.

▶ *The date of incorporation was Friday, June 14.*

▶ *Friday, June 14, 2019, was a special day.*

Quotation marks show which words are yours and which belong to someone else.

QUOTATION MARKS

Borrowing Words

DIRECT QUOTATIONS

Most commonly, quotation marks show readers the exact words someone said, in the exact order they were said.

She told her student, "Keep your eyes on your own paper."

DIALOGUE

Quotation marks are used in written dialogue to capture a conversation. Use them to open and close each speaker's contribution.

Anna said, "Your phone is ringing."
"I'll get it," John said, "right after I find my keys."

QUOTING SOURCES

When quoting from a source, enclose all quoted material in quotation marks.

The text said, "I'll be at the park at 6:00 p.m., but I won't wait longer than an hour."

TITLES

Quotation marks are also used for titles of short works, such as short poems, short stories, newspaper or magazine articles, book chapters, songs, and TV show episodes.

Her mother's favorite poem was "The Road Not Taken" by Robert Frost.

SLANG OR TECHNICAL TERMS

Slang, jargon, and other words outside their normal usage can be put in quotation marks or italics.

Her grandma didn't know what "LOL" meant.

GOOD TO KNOW:

PUNCTUATION AND QUOTATION MARKS

Periods and commas always go inside closing quotation marks. Colons and semicolons go outside closing quotation marks. If a question mark or exclamation point was originally part of the quoted text, the punctuation mark goes inside the closing quotation mark; if it was not part of the original quote, it goes outside the closing quotation mark.

COLONS & SEMICOLONS

Proper Punctuation: Introducing and Connecting

Semicolons indicate a pause that is more significant than a comma but less significant than a period. Most often, they connect two complete thoughts that could be two separate sentences but are logically connected.

> *I rode to town on my horse.*
> *He started out at a trot.*
>
> *I rode to town on my horse;*
> *he started out at a trot.*

Semicolons can also stand in for commas when clearer punctuation is needed.

> *The contest winners came from Sacramento,*
> *California; Nashville, Tennessee; and Tulsa, Oklahoma.*

Colons

Colons introduce more information. These must be used after an independent clause, but what they introduce may not always be a complete sentence.

She knew my favorite foods: chocolate and peanut butter.

If the material after the colon is a complete sentence, capitalize the first letter.

They were committed: It would take seven weeks to hike overland to the base of K2.

WHEN TO USE A COLON

In a business letter greeting.
› *Dear Colleague:*

Between the hour and minutes in time.
› *4:30*

To divide a title and subtitle.
› *Frankenstein: The Modern Prometheus*

To name a chapter and verse of the Bible.
› *John 3:16*

HYPHENS, EM DASHES, &EN DASHES

WORD DIVIDERS

HYPHENS and **DASHES** separate words and thoughts. A **HYPHEN** is **shorter**, while **EN** and **EM DASHES** are **longer**.

USING HYPHENS

HYPHEN

In general, use a **HYPHEN** to:

1 Create compound adjectives.

EXAMPLES
twentieth-century, ready-made

2 Spell out numbers.

EXAMPLE
sixty-four

USING DASHES

EM DASH

An **EM DASH** —which is the longest dash—introduces a sudden idea or gives more information.

EXAMPLES

1. The entire group—consisting of boys, girls, and chaperones—purchased tickets.

2. I found my notebook in the car—a great relief after weeks of searching.

EN DASH

An **EN DASH** is used to show a range, such as spans of time or page numbers.

EXAMPLE

The American Civil War (1861–1865) pitted brother against brother.

 GOOD TO KNOW:

NO HYPHEN NECESSARY

Don't use a hyphen when the modifier preceding the noun contains an adverb ending in -*ly*.

EXAMPLE: The highly regarded teacher won the award.

Enclosing Extra Information

{ **Parentheses** set off extra information—material that may not be necessary (but can be helpful). }

USES

{ ### Setting Off Part of a Sentence

Use parentheses when you want to set off a word or phrase from the rest of the sentence. The parentheses show that the word(s) inside could be omitted without affecting the sentence's meaning.

I chose the spiciest chili powder and used plenty of it (though I'm not sure that Janie liked it). }

Dates

Enclose dates and date ranges, like for birth and death dates or historical eras (and remember to use an en dash).

George Washington (1732–1799) was the first American president.

123...

Series

Use parentheses when writing about items in a series using numbers or letters.

I told the students to (a) break into groups, (b) choose a team leader, and (c) begin working.

Political Affiliations

Politicians' party affiliation and home state, city, or county are enclosed in parentheses.

Senator John Smith (D-MA) entered the race.

Alternate Endings

A letter or letters in parentheses at the end of a word indicate an alternate ending.

Please make sure to tell your child(ren).

BRACKETS

Square brackets are most commonly found in dictionaries, where they enclose the history of the word being defined. Other than this usage, there are a few key places where you'll find them.

Parentheses and brackets always come in pairs, with an opening mark and a closing mark.

In Quotations

You'll often find square brackets in quoted passages when the use of a pronoun needs clarification. The brackets show that the enclosed text is not part of the original quote, and their use should not change the sentence's meaning.

"She [Catherine, Duchess of Cambridge] is known for her commitment to charitable causes."

Inside Parentheses

Use brackets when you'd normally use parentheses but the words are already enclosed.

The cofounder of the suffragist movement (Susan B. Anthony [1820–1906]) pushed for the Nineteenth Amendment.

To Point Out a Mistake in Quoted Text

On very rare occasions, you'll use brackets to indicate that material you're quoting has a mistake, but you're not correcting it. The designation "[sic]" acknowledges the mistake and explains it's not yours.

"The event took place on April 31 [sic]."

Sic means "so" or "thus" in Latin and is used in brackets to note "this is the way the text really appears."

BOLD, *Italics,*

Bold, *italics,* and <u>underlining</u> all emphasize words. Although you should use these elements sparingly, here's when to use them:

Titles

EMPHASIS

Foreign Words & Written Sounds

 GOOD TO KNOW:

ITALICIZING PUNCTUATION

Commas, periods, exclamation points, question marks, and other forms of punctuation are only italicized if they are part of a work's title.

and <u>Underlining</u>

The names of movies, books, poem collections, plays, operas, TV shows, works of art, magazines, newspapers, ships, aircraft, spacecraft, and trains are all *italicized*.

Example:

We rode Amtrak's *City of New Orleans* back to Chicago.

Use <u>underline</u> when you're writing titles by hand.

Example:

We saw <u>Hamlet.</u>

To emphasize certain words, you *italicize* them. Sometimes, especially in graphic design, **bolding** will be used.

Example:

I *certainly* didn't know **that**.

Words from another language are *italicized*. So are onomatopoeia, or written sounds.

Examples:

My mom will be *chez moi*.

Brr, it's really cold!

Examples:

Did you see *A Raisin in the Sun*?

Who's Afraid of Virginia Woolf? is a great play.

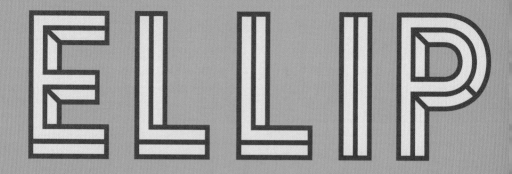

ELLIP

An **ellipsis** is a punctuation mark comprising three dots (periods) with no spaces between them.

Ellipses have two main functions:

- To signal word omission from a quoted passage
- To express mood

SPACES AND ELLIPSES

Style guides and teachers don't always agree. Sometimes ellipses are followed by a space, and sometimes they're not. To complicate matters, some style guides combine a period and ellipsis to show that the sentence before the omitted text was complete.

OMISSION

To save space, use an ellipsis when cutting out a word or phrase that isn't relevant to the meaning of the material you're quoting.

EXAMPLE:

"Yesterday, while doing something else, I found her car keys."

"Yesterday...I found her car keys."

MOOD

An ellipsis can express uncertainty or suspense, or indicate a thought is trailing off.

EXAMPLES:

I'm not sure about this...

What would you do if...?

THE SLASH

The slash has four main uses in writing.

1 / URLs

Separates portions of the address in a URL.

https://nps.gov/state/ak

2 / Or

Stands in for *or*.

Students may bring their mothers/fathers to the open house.

3 Per

Stands in for *per* when discussing units of measure.

The rate of ascent was 500 feet/hour.

4 Fractions

Expresses partial numbers.

Add ¾ cup of milk.

DID YOU KNOW?

The slash is also called a ***virgule*** or a ***solidus*** and dates back to Roman times.

The English language is chock-full of **abbreviations** and acronyms, which are shortened words or phrases.

MR.
Mister

ABBREVIATIONS

An *abbreviation* is a series of letters that serves as a shortened version of a longer word. You still read or speak the full word.

DR.
Doctor

ST.
Street

DID YOU KNOW?

Abbreviation comes from the word ***brevis***, which is Latin for "short."

PRES.
President

DIY
Do it
yourself

& ACRONYMS

An *acronym* is a new word formed by the
initial letters of the words it comprises.

ASAP
As soon as
possible

BLT
Bacon, lettuce,
tomato

CHAPTER 4

WRITING STYLE

Identifying Your Purpose and Audience 84

Active & Passive Voice 86

Using Transitional Words and Phrases 88

Paragraph Structure 90

Fixing Repetition and Introducing Variety 92

Foreign Words & Phrases 94

Slang & Dialect 96

Improving Writing 98

Style Guides: A Brief Overview 100

IDENTIFYING YOUR PURPOSE AND AUDIENCE

Content and Connection

Knowing your specific audience will guide what you write and the words you use.

Determine Purpose

Most writing aims to reach, educate, or persuade.
Be specific: Are you making a case for why your curfew should be extended? Explaining the origins behind the ancient city of Machu Picchu?
Ask yourself: *What is my goal?*

Identify Your Audience

Who will benefit from or be persuaded by your writing?
Again, be specific.
Ask yourself: *Whom am I talking to?*

Consider Content

What will make your writing believable or persuasive?
Recent research? Numbers and statistics? Direct quotes?
Ask yourself: *What do I need to make sure readers know? What facts will persuade them?*

Decide On Definitions

If you're including jargon or technical terms, do you need to include definitions?
Ask yourself: *Will my readers know what I'm talking about?*

Create Connection

Think of a suspenseful story or a passionately argued opinion-editorial column: Using the right voice and tone can create a specific mood.
Ask yourself: *How would I talk to my audience in person?*

Call to Action

Are you asking your audience to do anything at the end of your writing? Learn more? Consider the issue? If so, include a *call to action*.
Ask yourself: *What should my audience want to do after reading my writing?*

Active & Passive Voice

Voice: Expressing Action

Sentences with action verbs and direct objects can be written in *active voice* or *passive voice*. Understand the difference between the two.

A Quick Refresher

▶ An *action verb* shows movement or change, rather than a state of being.

▶ A *direct object* receives the action of the verb.

ACTIVE VOICE IS CLEARER

A sentence in active voice is easier to understand than the same sentence in passive voice. Use active voice whenever possible to make your writing crisp, clear, and direct.

Active Voice

The subject is in charge. It performs the action of the verb.

Example:
The boy threw the ball.

Passive Voice

The subject isn't in charge. Instead, it is acted upon by the verb, and the direct object becomes the subject.

Example:
The ball was thrown by the boy.

Converting
Passive Voice to Active Voice

1. Look for the prepositional phrase; that's where you're likely to find your subject. In the previous example, it's *by the boy*.

2. Remove the auxiliary verb: *was*.

3. Correct the verb tense: *thrown* becomes *threw*.

4. Make the subject the direct object: *the ball*.

5. **Final:** *The boy threw the ball*.

SING TRANSITIONAL ORDS AND PHRASES

	USAGE
123	To show sequence or explain steps
⫸	To indicate cause and effect
⚖	To compare
◐	To contrast
✚	To show addition or emphasis
🕘	To indicate time
Ⓒ	To generalize
📍	To show place
👍	To indicate exceptions or signal concession

We learn to speak when we're really young, so talking often comes naturally. Sometimes writing doesn't. Use transitional words and phrases to keep your sentences and paragraphs flowing.

EXAMPLE WORDS

first, second, before, after, then, afterward, next, as soon as, still, furthermore, last, finally

therefore, thus, as a result, so, since, consequently

similarly, actually, indeed, likewise, in fact

however, nevertheless, on the one hand, on the other hand, despite, still, regardless

besides, also, furthermore, in addition, another, moreover

before, during, after, while, earlier, later, after a bit

generally, in general, typically, usually

above, below, beyond, in front of, behind, lower, higher

of course, no doubt, sure, naturally, certainly

PARAGRAPH STRUCTURE

Paragraphs with Purpose

A paragraph is a group of sentences united by a single topic or point. Knowing how to construct a paragraph will help you write coherently and persuasively.

In general, there are
3 TYPES of paragraphs:

1. INTRODUCTORY
2. BODY
3. CONCLUDING

INTRODUCTORY PARAGRAPHS:

explain the why, what, and how of your writing. They include:

- A hook, which snares your audience's attention
- A thesis explaining your position or the point of the article, paper, etc.
- A transition telling your audience what to expect next

BODY PARAGRAPHS:

provide evidence. They:

- Introduce the point of the paragraph
- Provide evidence or examples to support your point
- Offer a transition to the next paragraph (remember, use transitional words!)

CONCLUDING PARAGRAPHS:

summarize. They:

- Restate your thesis and the points you've made
- Help your readers understand what you want them to take away
- May include a call to action

FIXING REPETITION
AND INTRODUCING
INTRODUCING
VARieTy

Making Writing Sparkle

Clarity is important in writing, but so is variety. Keep your readers interested by avoiding repetition in sentence length and word choice.

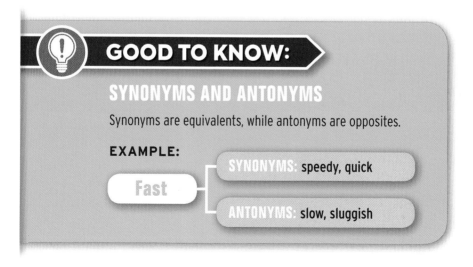

GOOD TO KNOW:

SYNONYMS AND ANTONYMS

Synonyms are equivalents, while antonyms are opposites.

EXAMPLE:

Fast
- **SYNONYMS:** speedy, quick
- **ANTONYMS:** slow, sluggish

DID YOU KNOW?

A thesaurus expands your vocabulary with synonyms and antonyms. You can find online and print versions.

SENTENCE LENGTH

Remember the four basic types of sentences: simple, compound, complex, and compound-complex? Express your thoughts in a variety of sentence types to keep your reader engaged.

- **SHORT SENTENCES**
  add emphasis or contrast.

- **LONGER SENTENCES**
  keep your ideas flowing.

(For a refresher, see Sentence Functions in Chapter 2.)

SENTENCE VARIETY

You can make your writing more interesting and engaging by including a variety of sentence types in each paragraph. Vary the length, complexity, and word choices in your sentences to keep your content from sounding too repetitive. For example:

She looked at the clock.
(simple sentence)

*If she didn't hurry,
she would miss the train.*
(complex sentence)

*The tickets were sold out,
and it was her only chance to
get home for the holidays.*
(compound sentence)

SENTENCE VARIETY

Foreign Words

English is a language of borrowed words, with influences from German, French, and many other tongues. When using foreign words and phrases, how do you write them?

French:
Faux Pas

Nahuatl/Aztec:
Tomato

German:
Angst

ℹ ITALICIZE

Put the foreign word in italics when it is:

- *Unfamiliar or requires a definition*
- *Used for the first time*
- *A single word or a brief phrase*

ℹ DON'T ITALICIZE

Italics aren't necessary when the word is:

- *Familiar*
- *Used again, after an initial italicization*

 & Phrases

LOCAL CULTURAL INFLUENCES

Depending on where you live, cultural and linguistic influences may play a role in what is familiar or not familiar. For example, Texans know Tejano music, so there is no need to italicize Tejano.

Russian:
Mammoth

Sanskrit:
Avatar

Chinese:
Tea

Arabic:
Alcohol

💬 USE QUOTES

Using a direct quote from a foreign-language speaker or source?

- *Don't italicize*
- *Enclose the entire statement in quotation marks*

Ⓐ PROPER NOUNS

When using a foreign-language proper noun, **do capitalize**, but **don't italicize.**

Would you like champagne?
I got it in Champagne.

Slang & Dialect

Many Shades of Language

A shared language isn't spoken the same way by all its speakers. **Slang** and **dialect** are both variations in language, but that's where their similarity ends. Understand them better using the following guide.

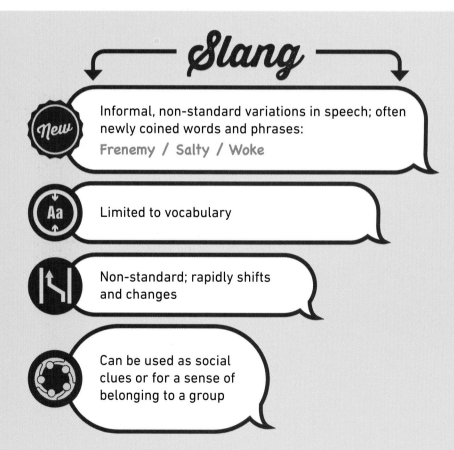

Slang

New — Informal, non-standard variations in speech; often newly coined words and phrases:
Frenemy / Salty / Woke

Aa — Limited to vocabulary

Non-standard; rapidly shifts and changes

Can be used as social clues or for a sense of belonging to a group

DID YOU KNOW?

The United States has no official language, though English is most commonly spoken.

Dialect

A variety of language spoken in a specific geographical area or by a specific group of people: Soda / Cola / Pop

Unique in vocabulary, grammar, and pronunciation

Can be standard or non-standard

Indicates a speaker comes from a specific geographical area

 GOOD TO KNOW:

Many Dialects There are more than twenty-five recognized dialects of American English, from North Midland to Gulf Southern—and more than one hundred additional English dialects spoken worldwide.

Improving

4 Tips to Improve Your Writing

Like any skill, your writing ability improves over time with practice. Here are a few tips that can help.

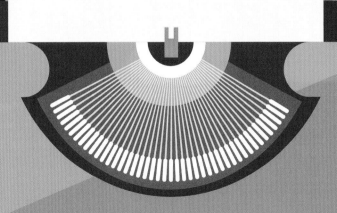

Writing

#1

READ GOOD WRITING

Fill your eyes and ears with good writing, and your own will improve. Read articles from such news sources as *The New York Times*, *The Washington Post*, and more. Choose novels and short stories that have received recognition or ask a local librarian for guidance.

#2

READ ALOUD

It's one thing to write words on a page and another to hear them spoken aloud. Your writing will have a more natural rhythm when it flows like you're talking. Get comfortable reading passages aloud to yourself or others.

#3

USE DIGITAL TOOLS

Most word processing programs, like Microsoft Word and Notes, come with a built-in spellcheck and grammar function, or you can download program extensions like Grammarly that flag common mistakes.

#4

RELY ON A PROOFREADER OR EDITOR

When it matters, ask for help. Writers and reporters rely on proofreaders or editors, and you can too. Ask a parent, teacher, or knowledgeable friend, classmate, or colleague to help.

STYLE GUIDES:
A Brief Overview

Establishing Standards and Rules

A style guide helps writers from very different backgrounds be consistent with grammar. There are several major style guides, and it's important to know which one your industry, academic institution, publication, or company prefers, as specifics of punctuation and citations vary.

 GOOD TO KNOW:

SPECIALTY STYLE GUIDES

If you're a student or scholar writing for the behavioral sciences, or you're a research doctor or medical scholar, you'll want to refer to the specialty guide for your industry, such as the APA (American Psychological Association) or AMA (American Medical Association) style guides.

Professional Writing and Editing

AP Style (Associated Press)

▸ **General usage:** newspapers, magazines, and public relations

▸ **Guidelines:** punctuation, abbreviations, and how to write names, dates, and addresses; also covers other "mechanics of style," such as spelling, capitalization, and treatment of numbers

Chicago Manual of Style

▸ **General usage:** writers, editors, proofreaders, indexers, copywriters, designers, and publishers

▸ **Guidelines:** bibliographies, citations, grammar, style, and word usage

Academia and Research

Turabian

▸ **General usage:** students, researchers, and based on the *Chicago Manual of Style*

▸ **Guidelines:** bibliographies and citations

MLA (Modern Language Association)

▸ **General usage:** high school students, scholars, journal publishers, and academic and commercial presses

▸ **Guidelines:** source citations, especially to avoid accusations of plagiarism

CHAPTER 5

COMMON MISTAKES

Clichés, Generalizations, Platitudes, and Jargon   104

Commonly Confused Words   106

Who & Whom   108

More Common Mistakes   110

Commonly Misused Phrases   112

Modifier Problems   114

Run-On Sentences and Wordiness   116

Double Negatives   118

Fussy Grammar   120

CLICHÉS, GENERALIZATIONS, PLATITUDES, AND JARGON

WORDS OF CAUTION: Tips for Avoiding Traps

There's as much magic in knowing the right words to use as in knowing which ones to avoid. Familiarize yourself with the common traps shown here and the tips to keep them out of your writing.

CLICHÉS

These worn-out, overused expressions can make your writing feel stale and overly simple.

Example: *She felt like a million bucks.*

! **QUICK TIP:** Use clichés in your first draft but find a more original way to express the • same idea in your second and final drafts.

GENERALIZATIONS

These are broad statements made about a group of people or things. Often, they're not true—and they can be offensive.

Example: *Politicians are greedy.*

QUICK TIP: If a statement is really broad or begins with "all," you might be making a generalization.

PLATITUDES

These are statements of the obvious, said as if they were new ideas.

Example: *Just be yourself.*

QUICK TIP: As with clichés, you can usually find a more original way to express your idea.

JARGON

These are technical words or phrases specific to a particular industry or context.

Example:

I whiffed on my first shot off one yesterday, but luckily my partner let me take a mulligan.

(I missed my golf shot off the first hole yesterday, but luckily my teammate let me have a do-over.)

QUICK TIP: Be sure to define jargon terms if you're writing for an audience that won't know what they mean.

COMMONLY CONFUSED WORDS

LEARN THE DIFFERENCES TO AVOID MISTAKES

 GOOD TO KNOW:

Homophones are pronounced the same way but have very different meanings; for example, **eye** and **I**.

THEIR/THERE/THEY'RE

Don't let this trio of homophones confound you.

Their indicates possession by two or more people: **Their car is in the shop.**

There indicates a certain location: **I found the ball over there.**

They're is a contraction of "they are": **They're going to come over later.**

YOUR/YOU'RE

Your indicates possession: **That is your coat.**

You're is a contraction of "you are": **You're going with me.**

WHOSE/WHO'S

As with *your*, **whose** indicates possession: **Whose coat is that?**

Who's is a contraction of "who is": **Who's coming with me?**

Even native English speakers struggle with some words and expressions. Take the time to learn which word is right in which context, and you'll always choose with confidence.

ITS/IT'S

Its is for possession: *My device needs charging; its cord is on the counter.*

It's is a contraction of "it is"; remember to check if the sentence sounds rights when you substitute "it is": *It's snowing again.*

TOO/TO/TWO

Too is an adverb meaning "also": *Now she is sick too.*

It can also mean "excessively" or "very": *It is too cold.*

To is a preposition: *They're going to the store.*

It can also be an adverb: *She was unconscious for a moment but then came to.*

Two indicates the number: *She had two cookies.*

LOOSE/LOSE

Loose is an adjective describing something that is not secure or evading capture: *The dog is on the loose. I have a loose tooth.*

Lose is a verb: *We are going to lose the game.*

WHO &

Which Pronoun?

If you struggle to decide whether to use **WHO** or **WHOM** in writing and speech, just remember: **Who** is always the subject of the verb in the sentence, while **Whom** is the object. You can use the words **He** (subject) and **Him** (object) to help you figure out which to use:

WHO = HE and WHOM = HIM

 SUBSTITUTION

If you can substitute **HE** and the sentence makes sense, you should use **WHO**. If **HIM** makes sense, you should use **WHOM**.

Try it out with a question:

Original: WHO/WHOM is hungry?

Substitution: HE is hungry.

Conclusion: WHO is correct.

WHOM

SCRAMBLING

Sometimes it's less obvious, and you might need to pick the statement or question apart to make the correct choice between **WHO** and **WHOM**. Make a question into a statement, or a statement into a question, and use the substitution trick.

Make a question into a statement:

Original:
WHO/WHOM did you call?

Substitution:
I called **HIM**.

Conclusion:
WHOM is correct.

Make a statement into a question:

Original: The child **WHO/WHOM** is crying is on the bench.

Substitution: Is **HE** crying on the bench?

Conclusion:
WHO is correct.

MORE COMMON MISTAKES

These words **can also cause** confusion.

EFFECT/AFFECT

EFFECT is most commonly used as a noun meaning "result":
The boat ride had a bad effect on me.

AFFECT is most commonly used as a verb, and means "to impact" or "to produce a change."
The boat ride affected me badly.

HINT
You can use the acronym **RAVEN** to remember which word to use:

Remember: **A**ffect-**V**erb, **E**ffect-**N**oun.

FARTHER/FURTHER

Use **FARTHER** for physical distance you can measure:
How much farther is our destination?

Use **FURTHER** when you can't measure the distance:
Before we go any further, let's make sure we're clear.

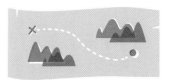

HINT
Remember, **FARTHER** contains **FAR**, so it is for distance you can measure.

GOOD/WELL

GOOD is an adjective and modifies nouns:
That was a good meal.

WELL is an adverb and modifies verbs:
She wasn't feeling well.
That meeting didn't go well.

FEWER/LESS

Use **FEWER** when you can count the items being discussed:
I have fewer apples than you do.

Use **LESS** when you can't:
She has less energy than I do.

FIGURATIVELY/LITERALLY

FIGURATIVELY makes use of a figure of speech:
I was figuratively thrown under the bus.

LITERALLY means "without exaggeration." Unless you were actually thrown under the bus, you cannot say *I was literally thrown under the bus.*

LIE/LAY

In the present tense, the **LIE/LAY** choice is pretty simple. You **LAY** something down, and people **LIE** down on their own. In the past tense, things get confusing, so memorize this table:

PRESENT TENSE	PAST TENSE	PAST PARTICIPLE
Lie	*Lay*	*Lain*
Lay	*Laid*	*Laid*

After hearing the news, I lay down on my bed.

I laid the book on the table.

COMMONLY MISUSED PHRASES

Language Traps: Confusing Phrases

Knowing the proper phrase and its spelling can go a long way toward improving your communication, whether it's professional or personal.

INCORRECT ✕

For all intensive purposes

One in the same

On accident

Tongue and cheek

Case and point

Should/could/would of

Mind your peas and cues

Make due

Tow the line

Nip it in the butt

Choosing the Right Saying

Have you ever heard or said, "I could care less"? The correct phrase is actually "I couldn't care less," because you're emphasizing that it is not possible for you to care less about the subject in question.

✔ CORRECT

- For all intents and purposes
- One and the same
- By accident
- Tongue in cheek
- Case in point
- Should/could/would have
- Mind your p's and q's
- Make do
- Toe the line
- Nip it in the bud

MODIFIER PROBLEMS
In the Wrong Place at the Wrong Time

When you're using modifiers, the words should be as close as possible to whatever they describe or elaborate on. Otherwise, mistakes can happen.

MISPLACED MODIFIERS

When a modifier is in the wrong place in a sentence, it can modify the wrong word.

Incorrect
We can't sell drinks to the attendees in glass bottles.

What?
The attendees are in glass bottles?

Correct
We can't sell drinks in glass bottles to the attendees.

LIMITING MODIFIERS

These words—which include *almost*, *even*, *hardly*, *just*, *merely*, *nearly*, and *only*—should be placed directly in front of whatever they're modifying.

Incorrect
We've nearly eaten a dozen cupcakes!

What?
Have you nearly eaten? Or have you eaten nearly a dozen?

Correct
We've eaten nearly a dozen cupcakes!

DANGLING MODIFIERS

These words don't have anything to hang on to in a sentence—they dangle.

Incorrect
Short of the goal line, the fans held their breath as the quarterback tripped.

What?
Why were the fans short of the goal line?

Correct
The fans held their breath as the quarterback tripped short of the goal line.

SQUINTING MODIFIERS

These two-way modifiers could describe a word on either side of them, so clarification is key.

Incorrect
Running up hills quickly strengthens your leg muscles.

What?
Does running quickly strengthen your muscles?
Or does it strengthen your muscles quickly?

Correct
Running quickly up hills strengthens your leg muscles.
(If "quickly" describes the speed of running.)

Running up hills strengthens your leg muscles quickly.
(If "quickly" describes the speed of muscle strengthening.)

RUN-ON SENTENCES

AND WORDINESS

Too Many Words

Contrary to their name, run-on sentences aren't necessarily long. In fact, they can be short. A run-on is a sentence that contains two or more independent clauses that are not joined properly. Usually, a punctuation mark or conjunction is needed to fix the problem.

Quick Tip: Remember, sentences need to be complete thoughts.

Example:

Dave brought his own lunch we bought hot lunch.

3 Ways to Solve Run-On Sentences

1. **Insert a period:** *Dave brought his own lunch. We bought hot lunch.*

2. **Use a semicolon:** *Dave brought his own lunch; we bought hot lunch.*

3. **Add a conjunction:** *Dave brought his own lunch, **but** we bought hot lunch.*

When you use more words than necessary, your writing is wordy. Wordiness can result from overly long transitional phrases or too much use of passive voice.

Keep It Short

Instead of ***due to the fact that*** ▸ use ***since*** or ***because***.

Instead of ***last but not least*** ▸ use ***finally***.

Instead of ***a small number of*** ▸ use ***a few***.

Instead of ***the majority of*** ▸ use ***most***.

DOUBLE NEGATIVES

Two Wrongs Don't Usually Make a Right

A double negative combines the negative form
of a verb with a negative pronoun,
adverb, or conjunction.

- **Negative Verb Forms:**
  cannot, did not, have not

- **Negative Pronouns:**
  nobody, nothing

- **Negative Adverbs:**
  never, hardly

- **Negative Conjunctions:**
  neither/nor

GOOD TO KNOW:

WHAT ABOUT "AIN'T"?

This contraction—meaning *am not*, *is not*, *are not*, *has not*, or *have not*—is centuries old. While it's considered unacceptable in formal writing, *ain't* peppers spoken English from time to time. You'll see it or use it when quoting a source or when you want to sound folksy.

"I ain't telling you anything you want to know, Sheriff!"

✖ When They're Wrong

Most of the time, a double negative is grammatically incorrect.

I didn't see nothing
should be ▶ *I didn't see anything.*

She didn't have neither vanilla nor chocolate should be ▶ *She didn't have either vanilla or chocolate.*

✔ When They're Right

Sometimes, a double negative lets a speaker speak factually—but not in a complimentary way. These are correct but awkward sentences.

She isn't unqualified.

He isn't unattractive.

FUSSY GRAMMAR

Throughout life, you'll encounter situations in which total grammatical accuracy is in your best interest. These instances include formal writing assignments, such as school papers, exams, and published work, and other high-stakes situations, such as cover letters and job applications.

To whom it may concern

This alternative to the salutation *Dear Sir or Madam* in a piece of formal correspondence should always use *whom*.

Between you and me

Why wouldn't you say *between you and I*? The reason is that *between* is a preposition, and it requires an object pronoun, in this case *me*.

There are other instances in which you'll encounter fussy grammarians who expect only the finest in sentence construction from you. Be prepared with this final roundup of correct expressions.

Toward vs. Towards

Drop the "s." In American English, the proper spelling is *toward*, *beside*, *amid*, or *among*, not *towards*, *besides*, *amidst*, or *amongst*.

The reason is...

You say either *The reason is...* or *because* when explaining. *The reason is because* is redundant.

Since

Fussy grammarians will tell you that *since* refers to the passage of time. All other uses should be replaced with *because.*

First vs. Firstly

Use *first* without exception. You're enumerating a list or explaining steps. The same goes for *second* instead of *secondly,* and so forth.

INDEX

A

Abbreviations, 80–81
Abstract nouns, 15
Accuracy, 120–21
Acronyms, 80–81, 110
Action verbs, 18–19, 86
Active voice, 52, 86–87
Adjective phrases, 46
Adjectives
    definite adjectives, 17
    demonstrative adjectives, 17
    indefinite adjectives, 17
    interrogative adjectives, 17
    modifiers, 16–17
    phrases, 46
    possessive adjectives, 17
    predicate adjectives, 45
    proper adjectives, 17
Adverb phrases, 46
Adverbs
    ending in -ly, 20, 69
    modifiers, 20–21, 69
    negative adverbs, 118
    phrases, 46
"Ain't," 119
Antonyms, 92, 93
Apostrophes, 60, 61
Appositive phrases, 47
Articles, 17
Attributive nouns, 15
Audience, identifying, 84–85
Auxiliary verbs, 18, 23, 87

B

Being verbs, 18, 19
Bold format, 74–75
Brackets, 72–73

C

Capitalization, 56–57
Clarity, 52–53, 92–93
Clauses
    commas with, 63
    dependent clauses, 31, 48
    independent clauses, 36–37, 48, 67, 116
    non-restrictive clauses, 50–51
    restrictive clauses, 50–51
    subordinate clauses, 36–37, 49
Clichés, 104–5
Collective nouns, 15
Colons, 65–67
Commas, 62–63, 74
Common nouns, 15
Complements, 44–45
Complete sentences, 36–37, 66–67, 116
Complete thoughts, 36–37, 48, 66–67, 116
Complex phrases, 48
Complex sentences, 37
Compound sentences, 37, 63
Compound subjects, 42–43
Compound-complex sentences, 37
Concrete nouns, 15
Conjunctions
    coordinating conjunctions, 30–31
    correlative conjunctions, 31
    negative conjunctions, 118

for run-on sentences, 117
   subordinating conjunctions, 31
Contractions, 60, 61, 119
Coordinating conjunctions, 30–31
Correlative conjunctions, 31
Correspondence, 120
Count nouns, 15

D

Dangling modifiers, 115
Dashes, 68–69, 71
Dates, 63, 71
Definite adjectives, 17
Demonstrative adjectives, 17
Demonstrative pronouns, 27
Dependent clauses, 31, 48
Dialect, 96–97
Dialogue, 32, 64
Digital tools, 99
Direct object, 19, 44–45, 86–87
Direct quotations, 64–65, 95
Double negatives, 118–19

E

Editors, 99, 101
Effect/affect, 110
Either/or, 31, 43, 119
Ellipses, 76–77
Em dashes, 68–69
Emphasis, 53, 74, 88, 93
En dashes, 68–69, 71
Exams, 120
Exclamation point, 58, 59, 65, 74

F

Farther/further, 110
Fewer/less, 111
Figuratively/literally, 111
First/firstly, 121
Foreign words/phrases, 74, 94–95
Formal writing, 120
Fractions, 41, 79
Future tense verbs, 22–23

G

Generalizations, 104–5
Gerunds, 47
Good/well, 111

H

He/him, 108–9
Homophones, 106
Hyphens, 68–69

I

Imperative sentences, 39
Incomplete sentences, 36, 57
Indefinite adjectives, 17
Indefinite pronouns, 27, 40, 41
Independent clauses, 36–37, 48, 67, 116
Indirect object, 45
Infinitive phrases, 47
Infinitive verb forms, 24–25
Interjections, 32–33
Interrogative adjectives, 17
Intransitive verbs, 19
Irregular verbs, 24–25
Italics, 74–75, 94
Its/it's, 61, 107

J

Jargon, 65, 85, 104–5
Job applications, 120

L

Letters, writing, 120
Lie/lay, 111
Limiting modifiers, 114
Linking verbs, 18, 45
Linking words, 28–29
Logical sentences, 52–53
Loose/lose, 107

M

Measurements, 41, 79, 110
Me/I, 120
Misplaced modifiers, 114–15

Mistakes
    clichés, 104–5
    confused words, 106–7
    double negatives, 118–19
    effect/affect, 110
    either/or, 31, 43, 119
    farther/further, 110
    fewer/less, 111
    figuratively/literally, 111
    first/firstly, 121
    fussy grammar, 120–21
    generalizations, 104–5
    good/well, 111
    he/him, 108–9
    its/it's, 61, 107
    jargon, 65, 85, 104–5
    lie/lay, 111
    loose/lose, 107
    me/I, 120
    modifiers, 114–15
    neither/nor, 31, 43, 118–19
    phrases, 112–13
    platitudes, 104–5
    run-on sentences, 116–17
    sayings, 112–13
    since/because, 121
    their/there/they're, 106
    too/to/two, 107
    toward/towards, 121
    which/that, 51
    whose/who's, 106
    who/whom, 108–9, 120
    wordiness, 116–17
    you/you're, 106
Modifiers
    adjectives, 16–17
    adverbs, 20–21, 69
    dangling modifiers, 115
    limiting modifiers, 114
    misplaced modifiers, 114–15
    squinting modifiers, 115

N

Negative adverbs, 118
Negative conjunctions, 118
Negative pronouns, 118
Negative verb forms, 118
Negatives, double, 118–19
Neither/nor, 31, 43, 118–19
Non-count nouns, 15
Non-restrictive clauses, 50–51
Nouns
    abstract nouns, 15
    attributive nouns, 15
    collective nouns, 15
    common nouns, 15
    concrete nouns, 15
    count nouns, 15
    explanation of, 14–15
    non-count nouns, 15
    possessive nouns, 15
    proper nouns, 15

O

Objects
    direct object, 19, 44–45, 86–87
    indirect object, 45
    object complement, 44–45
    object pronoun, 120

P

Paragraph structure, 90–91
Parallelism, 52–53
Parentheses, 70–71
Participial phrases, 47
Parts of speech
    adjectives, 16–17, 45–46
    adverbs, 20–21, 46, 69, 118
    articles, 17
    conjunctions, 30–31, 117–18
    interjections, 32–33
    nouns, 14–15
    prepositional phrases, 28–29, 41, 87
    prepositions, 28–29

pronouns, 26–27, 40–41, 118, 120
verb tenses, 22–23, 53, 87
verbs, 18–19, 23–25, 40–45, 86–87
Passive voice, 52, 86–87, 117
Past participle verb forms, 24–25
Past tense verbs, 22–23
Period, 58, 74, 117
Personal pronouns, 27
Phrases
adjective phrases, 46
adverb phrases, 46
appositive phrases, 47
complex phrases, 48
foreign phrases, 74, 94–95
infinitive phrases, 47
misused phrases, 112–13
participial phrases, 47
prepositional phrases, 28–29, 41, 87
transitional phrases, 88–89
Platitudes, 104–5
Plural pronouns, 41
Plural subjects, 42–43
Plural verbs, 40–43
Plurals, forming, 60, 61
Possession, indicating, 60
Possessive adjectives, 17
Possessive nouns, 15
Possessive pronouns, 27
Predicate adjectives, 45
Predicate nominative, 45
Predicates, 38–39
Prepositional phrases, 28–29, 41, 87
Prepositions, 28–29
Present particle verb forms, 24
Present tense verbs, 22–23
Pronouns
classifications of, 27
demonstrative pronouns, 27
explanation of, 26–27
indefinite pronouns, 27, 40, 41
negative pronouns, 118
object pronouns, 120

personal pronouns, 27
plural pronouns, 41
possessive pronouns, 27
reflexive pronouns, 27
relative pronouns, 27
singular pronouns, 26, 41
Proofreaders, 99, 101
Proper adjectives, 17
Proper nouns, 15
Published works, 120
Punctuation
abbreviations, 80–81
acronyms, 80–81, 110
apostrophes, 60, 61
bold format, 74–75
brackets, 72–73
capitalization, 56–57
colons, 65–67
commas, 62–63, 74
contractions, 60, 61, 119
ellipses, 76–77
em dashes, 68–69
en dashes, 68–69, 71
ending sentences, 58–59, 74, 117
exclamation point, 58, 59, 65, 74
hyphens, 68–69
italics format, 74–75, 94
parentheses, 70–71
period, 58, 74, 117
question marks, 58, 59, 65, 74
quotation marks, 64–65
semicolons, 65–67, 117
in sentences, 55–81, 117
slash, 78–79
underlining, 74–75

Q

Question marks, 58, 59, 65, 74
Quotation marks, 64–65
Quotations, 64–65, 72–73, 95

R

Reflexive pronouns, 27
Regular verbs, 24–25
Relative pronouns, 27
Repetition, fixing, 92–93
Restrictive clauses, 50–51
Run-on sentences, 116–17

S

Sayings, misused, 112–13
School papers, 120
Semicolons, 65–67, 117
Sentence fragments, 36
Sentence functions, 36–37
Sentence length, 92–93
Sentence structure
  clarity, 52–53, 92–93
  clauses, 36–37, 48–51, 63, 67, 116
  complements, 44–45
  complete sentences, 36–37, 66–67,
    116
  complex sentences, 37
  compound sentences, 37, 63
  compound subjects, 42–43
  compound-complex sentences, 37
  imperative sentences, 39
  incomplete sentences, 36, 57
  logical sentences, 52–53
  non-restrictive clauses, 50–51
  objects, 19, 44–45, 86–87
  parallelism, 52–53
  phrases, 41, 46–48, 87
  predicates, 38–39
  punctuation, 55–81
  restrictive clauses, 50–51
  run-on sentences, 116–17
  sentence fragments, 36
  sentence functions, 36–37
  sentence length, 92–93
  sentence variety, 92–93
  simple sentences, 37

  subjects, 38–43
  subject-verb agreement, 40–43
  wordiness, 116–17
Sentence variety, 92–93
Serial comma, 62–63
Simple past verb forms, 24–25
Simple present verb forms, 24
Simple sentences, 37
Since/because, 121
Singular pronouns, 26, 41
Singular subjects, 42–43
Singular verbs, 40–43
Slang, 65, 96–97
Slash, 78–79
Speech, parts of, 13–33. *See also* Parts
  of speech
Squinting modifiers, 115
Style guides, 100–101
Subjects
  compound subjects, 42–43
  explanation of, 38–43
  plural subjects, 42–43
  singular subjects, 42–43
  subject-verb agreement, 40–43
Subordinate clauses, 36–37, 49
Subordinating conjunctions, 31
Synonyms, 92, 93

T

Technical terms, 65, 85, 105
That/which, 51
Their/there/they're, 106
Thesaurus, 93
Titles, 41, 57, 65, 67, 74–75
Too/to/two, 107
Toward/towards, 121
Transitional words/phrases, 88–89
Transitive verbs, 19

U

Underlining, 74–75
URLs, 78

V

Variety, using, 92–93
Verbs
    action verbs, 18–19, 86
    auxiliary verbs, 18, 23, 87
    of being, 18, 19
    infinitive verb forms, 24–25
    intransitive verbs, 19
    irregular verbs, 24–25
    linking verbs, 18, 45
    negative verb forms, 118
    past participle verb forms, 24–25
    plural verbs, 40–43
    present participle verb forms, 24
    regular verbs, 24–25
    simple past verb forms, 24–25
    simple present verb forms, 24
    singular verbs, 40–43
    subject-verb agreement, 40–43
    tenses, 22–23, 53, 87
    transitive verbs, 19
Voice, active, 52, 86–87
Voice, passive, 52, 86–87, 117

W

Which/that, 51
Whose/who's, 106
Who/whom, 108–9, 120
Word processing programs, 99
Wordiness, 116–17
Words, confused, 106–7
Writing purpose, 84–85
Writing style
    active voice, 52, 86–87
    audience and, 84–85
    clarity, 52–53, 92–93
    content considerations, 84–85
    dialect, 96–97
    foreign words/phrases, 74, 94–95
    goal of, 84–85
    improving, 98–99
    paragraph structure, 90–91
    passive voice, 52, 86–87, 117
    purpose of, 84–85
    repetition and, 92–93
    sentence length, 92–93
    sentence variety, 92–93
    slang, 65, 96–97
    style guides, 100–101
    transitional words/phrases, 88–89

Y

You and me/you and I, 120
Your/you're, 106

GET GRAPHIC

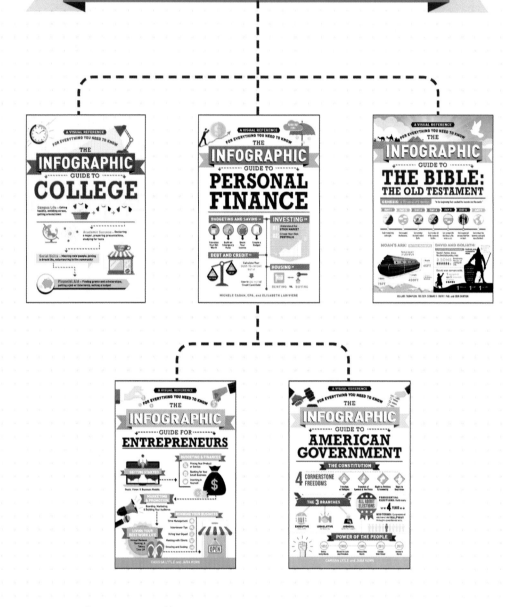

PICK UP OR DOWNLOAD YOUR COPIES TODAY!